area is in academics and teaching. Universities and colleges are finding opportunities to gain more students, increase their reach, and (as always) increase their bottom line by offering programs and classes online. In fact, new centers of academia are being created simply to meet the online student interest. For those who are comfortable working with a computer and the internet there is a great opportunity to get involved. Whether you are looking to share your

experience and knowledge, or to improve your income, teaching online offers to be a great source.

In 2006, USAToday reported that one in six students were taking some form of online courses. That is approximately 3.2 million people. (source: USAToday) We now live with a generation that has not experienced life without computers or the internet. These are people that maintain some type of connection (via computer, laptop. or web-enabled cell phone) to their friends, family, and others via some web service. Using the internet is a natural part of their being. With such demand, many universities and colleges are in need of faculty and staff who can teach online.

Some of the benefits to teaching via the internet are flexible scheduling, ability to work from almost anywhere, and to interact with faculty and students from far reaching locations. However, some of the setbacks can be continuous need to be up on latest technology, student expectations of contacting you almost anytime (day or night), and maintaining a reasonable work schedule (we will talk about this on another hub). There is no question though that teaching online can be very rewarding and the success stories can be endless.

So how do you begin teaching online for a college or university? First let's begin with a self assessment. What are your interests? What are you passionate about? What areas are your expertise? This is the starting point. Answer these and you will be well on your way to determining where you need to focus. As well, what is your academic education in? For many colleges, you will find you must at least have the degree equal or one above the one you wish to teach. Many universities will require a masters or doctorate to become faculty.

Second, you must develop a solid curriculum vita. This is very similar to a resume with a lot more depth and information. You must show your background in publishing, research, or speaking. If at this stage you do not have such experience, focus your information on your current skills sets and begin building the others. Remember, much like a traditional position, your resume/vita is your first contact. There are numerous resource, both online and in books, for developing a good vita.

Now, you've determined your area to teach and polished the resume/vita. Begin to research where you want to teach. Look for online universities that offer your program. Two websites that are excellent resources to begin are www.higheredjobs.com and

www.adjunctnation.com. AdjunctNation provides numerous resources for those that want to teach online or become "fulltime" adjuncts. As well, try to find organizations and associations in your field as these are great resources. Particularly if they have a website resource. This is a good starting point and will get you started. As you progress, you will begin to find others as well. As you do so, not them somewhere so that you can add those to your research list.

I hope this gets you started in beginning your online teaching career. As I've said, you will find teaching online to be a rewarding experience and very fulfilling. As well, remember, this is a starting point and an orientation. There are many ways to get started teaching and as you do your research, you will find many more. Good luck and enjoy the ride!

Writing a Great Curriculum Vita

Why a Vita...

In our last segment we talked about ways to begin teaching online. One of the elements of beginning such a quest is the curriculum vita. I found a very good article on the basics of writing a good vita in the article How to Write the Perfect Resume/Vita. This article provides some very good tips and suggestions for how to create one. The question I would like to address is, "How to

focus it for online." Keep in mind the vita is the first impression a potential employer will have of you. I've looked at a number of such, I can honestly tell you it does make or break the candidate. Keep in mind that colleges and universities look at numerous vitas throughout the year for positions they are hiring. As well, typically they are reviewed by a program coordinator, program chair, or hiring committee. Some of these people may be overwhelmed with other work and view the process as a necessary evil of the job. They are going to sort through the initial round fairly quickly to see who meets the needs of their department. Knowing such you can prepare yours to to move you through all levels of the hiring process.

There are some key differences between a resume and a vita. A resume is designed to be brief and to overview your background and accomplishments. A vita on the other hand is designed to provide a good understanding of your background, education, expertise, research, teaching background, and other pertinent information. With a vita, those hiring really want to get an indepth understanding of who you are and how you fit into their institution. Now this shouldn't overwhelm you by any means, nor should you stop now because you feel you do not have the background. All this means is that things you may not put on a resume, you must consider for a vita. (We will look at some ways to streamline updates and maintenance as well.)

What Should Be In A Vita...

While there are many variations to a vita, there are also some key elements that should be included. These are:

A Heading: Include your full name, address, contact telephone numbers, and email. (Remember: why would they hire someone to teach online who doesn't consider their email to be important contact information.)

14

A Skills Summary: Don't be shy here. Let them know what you are capable of, but keep in mind this is just a summary, so don't give them a dissertation. Just the highpoints here. Be sure to have keywords in here that relate to the position you are looking for (I'll explain later.)

Your Objective: It's ok to get a little philosophical here, but not too much. They want to know where you want to go in life, not the meaning of it. Again, be sure to use keywords for your area of interest.

Your Education: Let them know about your academic accomplishments, not just your degrees. While the workforce may not be interested in your award for "Best Weaver" in Basketweaving 101, schools will be. Also, show your GPA. If it was very good, it will be a selling point. If it was not, you might as well as they are going to find out anyway when they request an official copy of your transcripts.

Your Honors, Awards, and Accomplishments: Be sure to list them all. It is well worth the time trying to find all those certificates and letters to make sure you have the information correct.

Your Professional and Work Experience: Go into detail here. List your position, organization, duties, time there, and accomplishments with the organization.

Your Activities and Interests: Yes they are interested in that too. While it might sound like fluff, you never know when you might connect with a reviewer because of a shared hobby or interest.

Your References: Unless they request them with the paperwork, I usually put something like "References Available Upon Request". I do this for two reasons. First, it gives my references some privacy. I don't every place I send this too contacting my references unless they are really interested. Second, it gives me an idea if the school is really interested. If they call back for such, they must be. This isn't always the case, but it is a good indicator.

As far as formatting, I would find a good CV Book or an easier approach (and cheaper) is to do a search on the internet. There are thousands of experts and "claim-to-be" experts on writing CVs. If you do this though, don't just go with one site. Look over a number of them and particularly try to find patterns and consistencies between the sites. Where there is common ground, you will be in the ballpark. Again, there are many variations of a CV.

While this should be understood, do a spell check, grammar check, and have someone other than yourself read it. This will tell you if it makes sense. Preferably, a faculty member you may know that has served on such committees.

Ways to Stand Out...

Ok, so you have it all written, proofed, and you are ready to go. What next? Since you are going to be sending this out to interested positions, make sure you print it on good quality paper. Don't use something flashy, but don't use your copy paper either. A good bond paper with a neutral color will do fine.

Save your vita as a pdf. If you don't have Adobe Writer or a MS Word plugin, then download a free copy of OpenOffice. OpenOffice will import your MS Word document and then allow you to save it as a pdf. Even better, use OpenOffice to write your vita.

Finally, find a good hosting company, free blog site (without the advertisements), or similar. For blogging I recommend something like Blogger.com or something similar because they do not typically run ads. If you are looking investing in some reasonable hosting I would recommend IPower or Bluehost, because they are very reasonably priced and their hosting is very user friendly. Post your vita on there in a nice format. By doing so, you can also link to any sites you may have posted to such as Hubpages or the like. (If you haven't begun to do so... start posting some articles!) I'm not talking the family videos on YouTube or the annual family newsletter, but items that might draw attention for potential employers.

Remember those keywords I mentioned earlier. By doing this, your vita page will get bumped up on the search engines. You would be surprised how often folks will do a curiosity search for who is out there for a particular position. Wouldn't you like to be at the top of the list of the search results?

I hope this helps get you started. Certainly if I can be of assistance, contact me. The key is promotion and getting the point across that you are interested in teaching in their program and that you are the most qualified. Meeting these two, will take you far.

Seeking Out A University

Introduction

So far in our discussion we've overviewed becoming an online instructor or professor and how to create a great Curriculum Vita or C/V. What may be going through your mind now is, "now what?" In this segment, we will talk about three areas:

1. Scoping out the right online university
2. Building a relationship
3. Landing your first online teaching position

Working for an online university is much like a traditional one... you must be relational. So, if you are one of those folks that does not like to interact with people, you are going to struggle from here on out.

Scoping out the right online university

Previously, I asked you to consider your areas of expertise, your passions, and what subject areas you would thrive in. This is very important to understand who you are and how you work best. With this in hand, we are now going to begin matching up universities and colleges with your

information. I would consider what universities specialize in the area of my passion. Such publications as US News and World report put out an annual report of the top schools. One of the listings is by program and college. See which one's ranked the highest and make a list of them. You can also Google *top universities+your speciality*. Add to your listing this information from your search.

Finally, take a look at associations and academic websites related to your subject. Often you wil find academic programs referenced or mentioned. Add these to your list also. Once you have accumulated your list, mark off all the ones that do not offer an online program or courses. This should narrow down your search considerably. Remember we are wanting to teach online, not in a traditional classroom.

Now your list should be manageable. Consider visiting three sites:

1. HigherEdJobs.com
2. AdjunctNation.com
3. Indeed.com

HigherEdJobs.com is specifically for academics. Here you will find an enormous (almost overwhelming) listing of faculty jobs. Where you are going to focus your attention is on "Adjuncts" and "Online". At the top of the main page should be a link to adjunct/part time positions. You can also do a search for "Online Adjuncts". Browse through the lists (you can extend the list if needed) and look for positions with your interest. Write down the contact information and save the link to your favorites (I would suggest making a folder in your favorites for all of this to go to.)

AdjunctNation.com is similar, but when you come to the main page it might be a little overwhelming for some to navigate. No worries... look for the "Jobs" tab at the top. Enter your specialty in the search box, and click the online option in the box. Now you will see any jobs listed with your specialty and that are online. I would suggest also clearing the search box... click on the pull down option to choose your specialty and search. Sometimes schools do not word it in a way that the search engine picks it up correctly. Be sure to capture the information listed before.

Finally, Indeed.com is another site worth watching. The link I gave you above takes you to their faculty positions section. This will help get you started. Again, this site works like the others. Be careful though, as if you click the wrong links or something you are taken to the Indeed.com job void.

Now you should have a good solid listing of potential universities that are well known for your specialty. You've also saved them in a list to reference back to occasionally. Now we go to the next step.

Building a Relationship

Having a list is one thing, but making it work for you is critical. Begin by developing a solid cover letter. Overview you interest and passion for the subject. You should list (in an overview style) your professional experience, credentials, academic work, and so forth. I would recommend having someone read it to see if it makes sense, and sells you as a professor. Once you have a final draft, save this to your computer as you will be utilizing it quite regularly.

Now there are two schools of thought on the next part. One says that you should create a cover letter in a word processor and attach it to your email along with your vita. The second says that you should paste the cover letter in the email, then attach your vita to it. I tend to lean towards the latter. My thoughts are that when the reviewer gets the email, you have one shot to grab their attention before it goes to the trash folder, spam folder, or some file never to be found. It is really up to you though and what you are comfortable doing.

Using the information on your list, begin emailing the contacts that you wrote down in your job search. If there is something you do not understand or you missed, you can reference back to your web pages you saved to your favorites (you did save them didn't you?)

Make sure you have a solid email I would even recommend creating a standard intro email if you do not use your cover letter. Begin applying. Be sure to save your responses to a folder that you can find quickly. This way you can track who and who did not reply back.

Landing Your First Online Teaching Position

The best times to send out vitas and so forth, is usually around mid semester. The reason is that many colleges are pushed at the beginning to ensure students are ready

to go. At the end of the semester it is closing out classes, finalizing paperwork, and so forth. The midpoint seems to be when they have time to look at next semester's courses. This is the perfect time to let them know you are available and ready to go.

Do this at midpoint of every semester or quarter until you get offered a position, or they give a flat "No". Most are not offended by this as long as you do not overwhelm them with emails and calls. Just send a follow up once a semester. If you do more you annoy the hiring person and appear desperate.

With persistence, you will get an interview. Be sure to ask such questions as:
· What are their expectations of instructors?
· Tell me about your Learning Management System.
· Where do adjuncts fit into the university's system?

Should it all go well, you will receive an offer. Do not panic if you do not hear within the next day or two. Sometimes it takes time for paperwork and so forth to work its way through the system. Once you have received an offer, then you can ask about such things a salaries and benefits. I would recommend waiting until they offer you position, because I do not think its appropriate to do so in the interview.

One of the questions I get regularly is how many offers should I accept. A lot depends on the course loads and the rigor of the college or university. With that said, I typically recommend four to five. The reason is that adjunct work changes regularly. Some semesters you will have a lot of courses, others you will have a very small load. By leveraging your colleges, you will find the peaks and valleys to be more tolerable. You do not want to overload yourself, but as well you do not want to go hungry teaching. So try to find the right mix and balance.

Ways to Tell if Your Online University is a Scam

The recent rise in online universities opens the door for many to complete their degree and academic work via the internet.Google "online degrees" and you get a whopping 28,300,000 results. This list includes everything from colleges and universities, to companies that have popped up to help facilitate your online learning experience. But the new frontier in education doesn't come without its challenges. Getting a degree online provides some amazing

opportunities for learning, but along with it come the scam with diploma mills, and other fraudulent degrees. Investigations into for-profit online universities over financial aid issues, recruiting, and student completion, are a hot topic for many. Recent media and federal investigations have brought the issue to the forefront. Whether you are a student of an online university, or looking to teach for one, the question must be raised, "Is my university a valid one or a scam?"

A very simple first step is to look at the domain name of the potential candidate for a university. The nonprofit Educause, administers domain names with the .edu suffix. These are only given to colleges and universities that are accredited by the Department of Education. Don't see .edu
in the domain name? Run
away and do so fast.
The pivotal way of to find
out is through accreditation.
Easy enough? Not so fast,
defining college
accreditation is a vague
term, and some colleges
and universities take

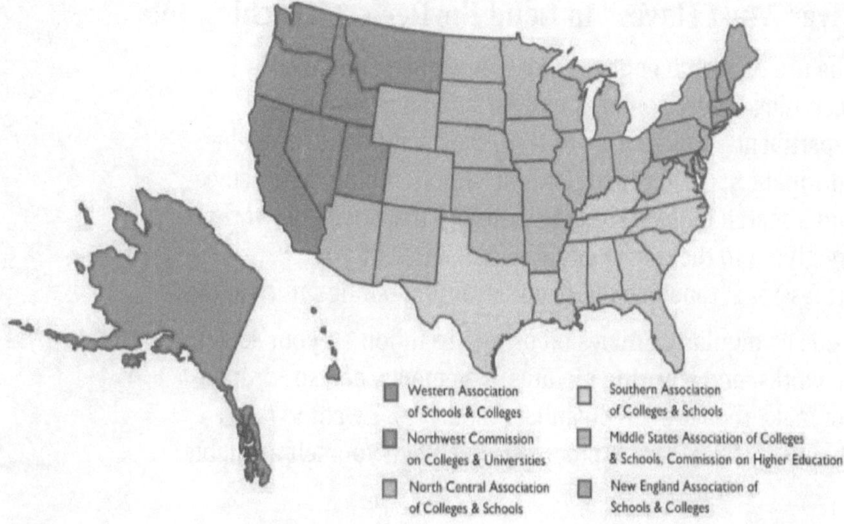

advantage of that. We can

narrow the field a bit by looking to see what the Department of Education recognizes for financial aid. According to the Department of Education, it recognizes over 6,900 postsecondary education institutions and programs . That helps some, but keep in mind you want your degree to be recognized academically. Suppose you want to go on for further academic work, study, or teach for a university. You are going to find that this is not enough and just using this list as your benchmark, some doors may still be closed.

The "gold standard" is the regional accreditation, and you should ensure that they are accredited by such. There are six associations that review the academic rigor of colleges and universities throughout the United States. This is not an easy process, and the work can be enormous. However, it ensures that the degree you are getting is valid and has met a minimum standard. Not having a degree from a regionally accredited university is selling yourself short.

Having a college degree opens many doors for you and provides opportunities that you may not, otherwise, have. Getting a degree from an online university provides a great deal of flexibility that a traditional one may not offer. The unfortunate side of the internet is that most anyone can set up a website and call it a university. Ensuring you have a valid degree will save you wasted time, money, and headaches down the road. A few simple steps in your investigation process may make all the difference in the world.

Five "Must Haves" to Land the Perfect Teaching Job

The use of search engines, like Google and Bing, are
becoming a very common tool for human resource
departments. It is so easy to learn the background, or gather
information, on job candidates by simply typing their name
into a search engine. Add the visibility that social networks
are giving to the search engines, and much of your
professional (and personal) are becoming public information.

You see regularly articles on using discretion on your social
networks, and ensuring pictures, statements, and so forth do
not make their way to potential employers. I want to talk
about ways you can be proactive and make yourself available

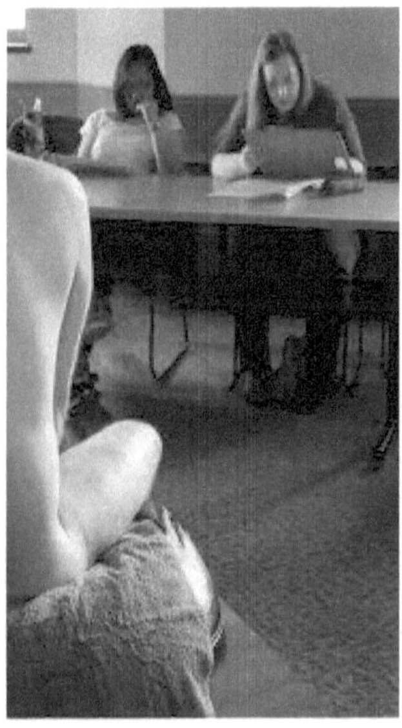

for potential jobs. While some HR departments may use
search engines for learning about applicants, some also use them to find
potential hires. So here are five things you can do to make yourself more
visible to them.

1. *Create an online resume or curriculum vita.* Too many people miss
opportunities because they are still using the traditional paper resume or CV.
If you haven't set up an online version, you are definitely missing out. The
easiest, and most user friendly I have found, is setting up a simpleWordPress
site (you will see why this is better further down.) Many hosting companies

provide this as an option for easy set up. It also has many features that will get you noticed on the web. I would consider adding features like All-in-one SEO and others. Do not go for a flashy or exotic theme, but look for something professional and represents how you want to be perceived.

2. *Add your professional experience, academics, publications, and accolades.* All of these go into a typical resume or CV. This is your time to shine and show them what you can really do. For experience, let them know your accomplishments and successes. Link to previous employers, to universities you have attended, and publications that may be available online. These links allow the headhunter or HR department to view exactly what you are listing. As well, any articles showing the awards and honors you have received, reinforce why they need to hire you.

3. *Provide links to videos and photos of you.* Now I would not recommend the photos of the all night party you and your friends have been bragging about for weeks, or that amazing video of the weird tricks your cat can do. Videos and photos of an amazing presentation or speaking engagement you did are perfect. What about those photos from a volunteer event that you were a part of? All of these build the character and show the depth of who you are. All become big pluses for someone looking for a candidate.

4. *Consider blogging.* Ok. Maybe you are not one of those folks that can hammer out 20 blog posts a day. However, seeing what your interests are, how you write, and what your views on certain issues may be, will be a huge asset. Through writing blog posts, the person gets an even better idea of how you approach issues, how you think, and what makes you tick. Many typically write like we talk, so it can be like an asynchronous interview. In the same token, make sure your posts are free of grammatical and spelling errors. Make these your best writing samples. Maintain this component and update it with fresh posts regularly.

5. *Add a portfolio.* A key selling point is seeing what you can do. If you have samples of your work, images, or others, consider putting them on your site. Proving you have an existing track record in the positions being searched, can put you miles ahead of other potential candidates.

It is no secret how competitive today's job market is. If you are competing for a position on the international market, the competition becomes even greater. Creating a well developed online resume or CV will put you well ahead of the competition. A well developed one will begin to bring the jobs and opportunities to you. I cannot begin to count the number of people who have told me they landed a high paying and rewarding position as result of being found online. Someone simply found them with a Google search or the like. Could that next person be you?

The Business Side of Being an Academic Free-Agent

When I first began working as an online instructor and contractor, some of the issues that came up were taxes, insurance, and so forth. This is a big issue for some and can be a deal breaker for many. There is a certain comfort level in knowing that you have your taxes paid, and that you have insurance for you and your family. I want to note that I am not an accountant, nor do I know the ins and outs of the tax law. However, if you are out there on your own, then here are some resources that may help.

First, for tracking your financial accounts, I would recommend something like Mint. Mint is a free, web-based software that runs from your computer or mobile device. It is very easy to use and setting up the system could not be easier. I also like that I can have it send me text messages when accounts reach a level, or if there is a sudden change. Make sure you remember your usernames, passwords, and secret questions when you set up your accounts, otherwise, you will have a hard time getting everything going. You can create budgets, set financial goals, and get a pretty good handle on where your expenses are going. It is not at all like Quickbooks, but if you are looking for a very simple financial management software, this is it.

Second, taxes are the one thing that trips many people up. You can get a very good accountant to help, but there may be some additional resources that may be beneficial. If you are not one to save for your taxes or just not a great saver in general, then consider a payroll management service. Now these can cover the gamet as far as services and products they provide. Basically, these services will allow you to sign up for free or close to free (check this in the interview, so as not to get any surprises.) You will need to set up a checking account with your bank for all your checks and receivables to go. You then establish your pay periods with the company, and they will withdraw the amount, take out your deductions, and provide you a check or direct deposit. Now most will attach a fee to this and it will vary. For example, the company I used, Paychex, to work with, charged $50.00 per paycheck, and $5.00 for direct deposit. Again, this will vary considerably from company to company, so do your research and interview the ones you are interested in. The payroll company then holds your taxes, and files them quarterly (they make most of their money by the interest accumulated while holding your funds until quarterly tax filing). At the end of the year, you receive your tax information, just as you would with a regular company. Many will also provide income tax filing for you the next year (most with some type of fee as well.) I have worked with bookkeepers, accountants, and others to do some of these things and the biggest headache was that I was still ultimately responsible for doing all the legwork. With many of the payroll companies, they handled everything. It ran on autopilot. However, you do want to pay close attention to the fees that go into the services. While you will find a lot of perks that will streamline your finances, be careful not to get overloaded with the associated costs. There was one additional perk that I really liked… insurance.

Many of us like the benefit of having medical and dental insurance. If you are supporting a family, this is a must. I have three kids and they pull the same crazy stuff, I used to as a kid. A good payroll service offers such benefits to their clients. The company collects a large number of small businesses, contractors, and even some mid-size businesses. They take all of these and negotiate discounted rates with the insurance companies. So you can get insurance, at times, at a very low rate and with many options. They will also work with you to set up a plan to reduce your insurance costs (including setting up a HSA). And guess what… it can be paid through your payroll deductions (pretax in some cases.) You can also set up retirement plans, 401Ks, and investment plans. Each year, they meet with you to make adjustments and changes that best suit your situation. In the situation I had, there were no fees attached to this from the payroll service. Now some of you may have read this and wondered, "why would one incur such an expense?" If you are a detailed business person, that can manage this on your own, I would congratulate you and ask you the same. However, I like to put as much on autopilot as I can, so I am not chasing so many details. My guess is some of you are the same. The important thing to do is careful homework with something like a payroll service. Interview their folks carefully and find out all the information you can. Get recommendations from your accountant, and ask for references of companies and people you can contact. With careful research and a little legwork on the front end, you can save yourself a significant amount of work and have peace of mind that you won't get any surprises.

How Many Contract Universities if Enough

I often get the question, "How many universities should I teach for as an academic free agent?" This is a tough question to answer, but I will show a few easy steps to determine what will work for you.

First, the most critical step in determining how many universities you should have as contracting is based on how much you want to make. I would suggest determining both your monthly and annual income need. Annual income gives you an idea of where to benchmark throughout the year. The monthly helps you determine more the day-to-day expenses. In addition, two times a year that I find teaching time is at its lowest are June and July, then again in November and December. You would want to factor in extra income during the months prior to such. You want to be completely honest here and ensure you have factored in ALL expenses, with some cushion in case of emergencies. (There are some helpful worksheets to do this in the Mobile Lifestyle Resources I have set up.)

Second, based upon your income determinations, you want to look at what the universities you have existing contracts are paying. If you are new to the Academic Free Agent, take a look at the guest post by Dr. Howard Rubin on How Much Do Professors Teaching Online Get Paid. You will find it to be a great starting point. Now consider the following. Some online teaching contracts pay per student, while others pay a flat rate. If your contracts pay per student, you will need to consider that student enrollment fluctuates, drop out rates, and so on when considering your income.

Finally, determine your availability. Now this may sound like a no-brainer, but life events come up, vacations, and many other things that may create time constraints. As well, it does not make sense to create a mobile lifestyle for yourself, only to spend your time locked away in your home office, or a hotel room, working away at all hours of the day and night. I find too many cases where people have ramped up numerous classes only to find themselves overloaded and unable to keep up. It is a sad, but true, story and the professor gets burned out and the students greatly suffer. As I said in a previous post, get a bad reputation at one or two universities and news travels fast.

With these notes in hand, you can begin determining what works best for you. In the book *Make Money Teaching Online: How to Land Your First Academic Job, Build Credibility, and Earn a Six-Figure Salary by Danielle Babb*, she recommends approximately four to five universities at one time.

This allows for classes being cancelled with some and changes to accommodate. That is great if you have no problems maintaining a class load when none cancel. I, typically, maintain three universities at one time. However, I am full-time at one, so I do not need to keep up as heavy a load. This allows me the time to ensure my classes are delivered properly and for any extra activities that may occur.

In addition, do not limit yourself to just teaching. Many universities and colleges have a need for course developers, project managers, and research coordinators. As well, there is a growing online market for tutors. So you can fill your time more effectively depending on the your schedule demands.

The key is to do your legwork upfront. Know what you need to bring in, some cushion for emergencies, and ensuring you can maintain the course load. Having a good balance will allow you to teach effectively and enjoy the freedom of living and working anywhere.

Ways to Manage Your Work
Six Ways to Streamline Your Life

Who isn't overwhelmed with all the things that go on during the day? There are so many things jockeying for our time, that sometimes it can be very overwhelming. Technology is great, but it is a double-edged sword. In one context it has certainly made our accessibility easier, but it has also made us more accessible to others. The internet has become much the same way. Between email, social networks, news, and information, just logging on to the net can generate feelings of anxiety and information overload. So what do we do to take control of the daily grind and flood of emails, cell phone calls, and various things that steal away our time. Here are a few things that can help.

1. Create a homepage: Google (iGoogle), Yahoo (Yahoo homepage), and Microsoft (MS Live), all have startpages that you can create for your browser. You can add items (also known as widgets), track news, and most anything else that draws your interest. The neat thing about these is that you can centralize all your important information such as your Calendar, Email, Chat, News, and most anything else that you find interesting.

2. Set up a Web Email Account: Much like the homepage, most of the search engines offer this for free. I personally use Gmail (by Google) because it is very good as removing spam and junkmail. Web email has really grown up from the days of just a simple browser based system. You can now centralize

all of your email account s (work, home, and others) into one location. Web email also offers the benefits of checking your email from anywhere, such as your cellphone, pda, or any computer with web access. I would suggest only checking your email three times a day. Many of us keep email open all the time and one would be amazed at how much time that eats away. Check it first thing in the morning, just before lunch, and at the end of the day. You will be amazed at how much time you free up, by setting limitations on email time. Centralizing your email will make this process easier. I would recommend only spending 30 minutes at a time checking and responding to email. If you feel really brave, only check it twice a day.

3. Set up a News Reader: A news reader (also known as a news aggregator) searches websites you designate for news and important information. With a news reader you can set up the various sites you find your news and it will consolidate it into one location. Now instead of having to go to the many websites you track, you can just go to one place. Click on the headlines you are interested in and skip the rest. You can also use these to research specific topics that you might use for a class or for some other need. Unless you are doing research for a class, I would recommend only checking this once a day. Spend about 30 minutes, depending on what your schedule permits.

4. Set up a Web-based Calendar: Much like the email, web-based calendars have really matured. You can track multiple calendars, share with others, and sync it with almost any type of software. You can also edit and manage one from a computer, cellphone, or pda. Also, reminders can be set to go to appear on your screen, ring your cellphone, or email you (but you are only checking your email a few times now...right?). I usually keep this up all the time (either on my homepage or in my browser). I can always reference my calendar at any time to keep up with meetings, deadlines, and so forth.

5. Turn off your phone: Telephone time eats up a lot of our day. Cellphones have made this worse. Let the phone go to voice mail and only check messages twice a day. The best times are at 11:30am and 4:30pm. This way you have time to return phone calls, but your day is not dominated by the calls.

6. Take Your Office Software to the Web: There are now about 20-30 excellent webbased office packages. Many of them free. By going to a web-based system, you can access your documents anywhere (even from your phone.) Think about how nice it would be to go into a class to teach, login to

a computer, go to the web and open your presentation. It's that easy.

All of the items mentioned here can be centralized onto your homepage. You can view and access your information at a glance. Items that might have required a lot of scanning websites, and working through mundane tasks, can now be automated. If you go this route, it does not matter which system you use, but I would recommend using the same for all. For example, if you set up Google for you homepage, use Gmail, Google Reader, Google Calendar, and Google Office. The reason I say this is that it will make integration easier and the various items will work well together.

Simplify, Simplify, Simplify…

This morning I took my dog for a walk (well one may argue that he took me out for a pull but none the less we had a morning out). He had to stop and check everything out by sniffing a plant here, trying some grass, and much more. I on the other hand was in a hurry to get to morning emails, classes, and so forth. However, as I reflected on the morning, I began to realize perhaps he has the better idea. Now I am not suggesting one go out and start chewing grass or sniffing weeds, but perhaps the simplicity of it all. There is a bit of irony in the world of technology that has transpired we have all missed. I remember reading a book by Bill Gates called "The Road Ahead". In this book he summarized the vision of the technology industry as well as Microsoft. The premise was that technology is a tool to simplify our lives and automate our mundane tasks giving us more freedom to be greater thinkers and innovators... in short to live life. However, what has become of this vision is the desire to plug more mundane in as we are able to do more. I believe we have missed the point. We should be capitalizing on the benefits of technology that we enjoy to remove the barriers that hinder enjoying life. Consider for a moment the amount of time you spend each day checking emails, returning phone calls, and other things that eat away at your day. My guess is you are probably thinking of a lot right now.

Here is a project I would recommend. Take one week and make very detailed notes of what you do each day. I would suggest at the minimum keep an hourly log and preferably more detailed. I know this sounds daunting but you will find it worthwhile in the end. After doing so for a week, sit back and review your listings. Amazing isn't it. My theory is that you will find that much of your hours are spent on things that are not the best use of your time. Don't feel alone in this as many of us do the same thing (myself included).

However, all is not lost and certainly being a slave to our tasks is not the end goal. So take a deep breath and read on.

The first step is the most complex. Looking through your list what are the things that are most important to you during the week. Someone once told me that the most important things in our week is not where we spend the most quantity, but where we spend the most quality. Just because email is the most time spent, doesn't mean it is the most important. Maybe its spending time with your kids or friends. Maybe its taking time to reflect and think of new ways to innovate your business. It is up to you what falls in this category,but these are your "uncompromisables". These are the absolutes that you want to ensure happen. Now get your calendar out or use your web calendar, and plug in times throughout the week where you want to focus on these. Ensure the times coincide for when you can actually do them. As well, these do not need to large amounts of time, just what you believe will be the proper commitment.

Now go back and look at the other items on your list. Let's chip away at the biggest time drainer of them all. For me it is email. My inbox fills up so fast that I almost feel obligated to check it often to ensure I am returning emails to everyone and getting back to them in a timely manner. However, what I consider to be a timely manner and what others do is different. Most business experts will tell you that emails should be returned in a 24 to 48 hour period. This is what they consider timely. If that is the case, then realistically you should only have to return email once a day. Not as bad as keeping the inbox open all the time to reply within minutes. So next is mark on your calendar when you will be returning email. For me it is first thing in the morning. I return all my emails, then shut it down for the day. Now I will admit I do have urgent emails go to my phone but beyond that I am done. Once you have completed your daily check, shut it down and force yourself not to reopen it. If you feel compelled to open something else like your Facebook page, at least there you are talking with friends and family rather than business.

Phone calls are another time killer. Throughout the day, I find my phone rings at all hours. Since I deal internationally, I will often get calls at night and in the early morning hours. I set up a virtual number to use for all my work related items. You can do this for free through Google Voice or any number of services. It's a very simple process and you can often have one within minutes. All calls (except the chosen few you decide) get this number to reach you. You then set it up for the times you are taking phone calls. An even simpler means is to have all calls roll to voice mail. You simply put on your message when you will be returning phone calls and when they can expect to hear from you. I would suggest checking this no more than twice a day and only during the week. Now mark the times you will be doing so in your calendar.

Finally, begin to review the other tasks that you are doing. What can be automated? What can be taken off your plate so to speak. You would be surprised how many software packages are available (and for free) to help with such. Do a search and see what you can find. As well, feel free to post a question here or email me. I am almost positive something can be found.

Now what you should find is that your time has significantly been freed up. It is very relieving isn't it? I would now set up a task list. I use the one in my Google Calendar but whatever works best for you is great. Make notes of the things that you need to get accomplished each week. Prioritize them so that you are not finding you are trying to fit them all into one day. Set dates to get them accomplished and follow it. You will find this will minimize the amount of time you are spending chasing from one project to another. So now you should find you have much more time focused to what you want to do. How do you fill the void? I know that sounds like a strange question considering what we've just talked about, but it will be a question that will come to mind. I would suggest taking at least a month before trying to answer this question. First, you want to get into a routine with your new schedule. Second you want to make sure that what you add to your week is really what you feel you need to do. Someone once told me that time is our true currency. We trade time for money, we trade time for relationships, and we trade it for the various things in our life. It is the one currency that doesn't lose value or depreciates. As well, we only have a limited amount of it. There is no adding more and we can only have less. How are you spending your currency? How are you spending the most precious commodity you have? Perhaps change is necessary to ensure you are investing it well.

Managing Online Office Hours

Teaching online has many benefits. You can work from anywhere and maintain flexible hours. However, it comes with some setbacks. It is not unusual to get phone calls at all hours of the day or night. I actually got a phone call from a student at 3am wanting help on a paper. As well, it is not uncommon to get the unexpected phone call that goes for an hour. While teaching online can be done at anytime during the day, so can the phone calls. Managing your time can become problematic. Here are some ways to manage office hours and maintain a personal life when being an online professor or instructor.

First, set very clear office hours. This is a must. However, you must make sure that it is a time that is available to your students. If, for example, I were to set my office hours from 8am to 12pm and my students are not available until 5pm… this is a problem. I open myself up to the unexpected phone call. Emphasize the office hours at the beginning of your class and throughout. Help students understand that you want to give full attention to their question or issue. By contacting you during office hours, you can provide your full attention.

Make sure you are available in those times. If you schedule meetings and personal errands during your office hours, and are unable to talk, you will find you will be contacted at other times. Keep your commitment to ensuring you are available.

Try using a scheduler for appointments with students. I use TimeDriver for mine and make sure students know it is available to schedule appointments with me. It is a webbased application that allows students to go in and see my availability, and pick a time that works for them. It has definitely proven to be a win-win for everyone.

Something I would highly recommend (and I mean HIGHLY recommend) is investing in a virtual telephone number. Now this may sound like overkill on the surface, but it pays off considerably. Virtual numbers are basically telephone numbers that you can create with a service. Most are fairly inexpensive. However, you can have it forward to any existing telephone you may have (ie, home phone, cellphone, hotel phone, etc.) This is great for the mobile person and working from anywhere faculty. Many will allow you to:

- Set parameters for when you will (and will not) receive phone calls
- Send calls to your existing location
- Receive virtual faxes
- Allow for conference calls (great for small study or review sessions)
- Caller ID to screen calls
- Voice mail (often that convert to text and email you)

There are an unlimited uses for having such. I started using a virtual number for my classes a few years ago and it has proven to work wonders. This is the only number I give out. (My personal number is only given out to a small close group.) I have the times to receive calls only during my office hours. Calls received otherwise are sent to voice mail. This has been an amazing tool, that has saved my an incredible amount of uninterrupted time.

If you were to do a search on companies that provide this service, you will find there are many. Some things I would look for would be:

- *Do they have a trial period?* They should at least give a period to try out the service to see if it is everything they say it is. If not, I would be concerned.
- *Are they reliable?*You don't want one that goes down frequently or does not have a clear sound. Calls that break up or have background noise is a big problem.
- *What type of support do they offer?* You should be able to call and talk to someone should you have problems.
- *Do they have set up fees?* Honestly, with competitive as this market is, you should not have to pay any.
- *Is there a call out feature?* It does not make sense for you to return a call

and your personal number comes up on their caller ID. Guess which number is going to get called next time?

· *Can I participate in conference calls?* Some conference call services will not allow for some of these services. They are blocked. Be sure your's works with your university's conference call system.

If you get a yes to all of these questions, and the price is reasonable, you have your service. While having a service such as this may cost you a monthly fee, think of it as more of an investment in your work. It will provide you with the freedom to work from anywhere, and eliminate the times where you are interrupted unnecessarily. You will definitely find that it is worth it's weight in gold.

If you are looking for a service, one I use and highly recommend RingCentral. It provides all the services I recommend and then some.

Outsource It and Relax

When I started up my online training company, I often found myself with too many tasks and not enough time. I am sure some of you reading this understand. In times when I needed to be thinking strategically, I was too busy trying to deal with the day to day. The reality is there just is not enough time in the day to deal with all the things that are going on in our personal lives and our professional. Enter Elance (www.elance.com). I have been using Elance for a few years now, and there have been many times they have saved me both time and money. Whether there was a project that I needed to complete quickly, or outsourcing some form of my personal life, Elance was there to help. In a nutshell, you post your project on the site and providers bid on them. Something like a contractor version of Ebay. This is oversimplifyingthough, so let's look at it in more specifics.

First you go to the site and create an account. This may take a few minutes, but it is not overwhelming by any means. Once your account has been set up and confirmed, you are ready to go to work (metaphorically speaking of course.) You have several ways you can look for a contractor. The first way is simply doing a search based on a keyword associated with your need. For example, you need someone to do research for a blog post you are writing. You can type in"blog research", or "research", and you will get a listing of individuals that do this type of work. Maybe you want someone to help you edit an article. Simply type in "copy edit" and you will get a listing of people who do so.

A better way of doing this i s to "Post a Job". You will find this under the "Hire" pull down in the dashboard. When you click the link, you will be taken to a web form that asks you to fill out the details of your job. Such things as a title (be very specific here), a description of what you are wanting (again, be very specific), how you want to pay for the work, and so forth. Follow the instructions and your job is posted within a few minutes on the site. From there, people can begin to bid on your project. This is very interesting, because you are not drawing interest from one location. People from all over the world will bid on your project. You will see their experience, qualifications, and credentials. You are provided a wealth of information about the person who wants to work for you. All of this, and a price comparison as well. When I have posted something work for you. All of this, and a price comparison as well. When I have posted something 15 bidders within the first day. Amazing… and all while I am doing other things.

Once the bidding is closed, or I have found the person I wanted, I am taken to a series of other screens to finalize the project. Elance has what they call an Escrow account that allows me to put the funds in holding while the person completes the project. Once I give the ok, Elance releases the funds. The potential contractor accepts the project, and we are off and going. Communication is critical, however, Elance provides an avenue for this through the project workspace. Once all is complete, I am asked to provide feedback on the person (they are also asked to provide feedback on me) and we part ways.

However, there are some helpful tips for posting jobs on Elance. First, the title and description needs to be very detailed and carefully worded. You want to make sure that the bidders understand what they are going to have to do. This will also reduce the time of going back and forth trying to explain what you want. It also reduces confusion in the end result. Elance also gives you the option of getting a upgraded listing. I rarely use this as I have found it really doesn't add any additional benefit. Save it for the big money projects you may have. You also want to be careful with your keywords. Make sure they are accurate to what you want. This is what Elance uses to make your listing searchable. You can use multiple ones, so take advantage of that.

Once the bids start coming in, do not jump at the first one or the cheapest. You will often find new bidders low-balling the bid to get the work. Elance sets a minimum bid of $50.00 USD. To jump at a bid, is a rookie mistake and one you may be sorry for later. Review the bidder's background, experience, and samples of their work. You may find that you will not be paying the lowest bidder, but the best qualified. It is well worth the extra bucks.

Agree to put the funds in escrow. This is a nice feature and definitely an incentive for the person working on your project. It ensures they are going to get paid, and many require that you do so before accepting the work. Once the work is complete, quickly release the escrow and provide feedback on the person. Feedback is critical for the contractors to get future work, so be honest, specific, and helpful.

So what type of projects have I used Elance for? Well I will give two examples. One that is work related and another that is personal.

Work Related

I posted a request for someone to copy edit an article I had written for a magazine. I posted on Elance the specifics, and within an hour received 10 replies. All had samples, credentials, and how they would go about the project. I let the posting go for the full 14 days, as I was not pushing a deadline for this one. What an amazing response, and I did not use the upgraded listing. I got a very qualified person to copy edit the article for $50.00 from Pakistan, and he said he could turn it around in about a day. Perfect! I posted the article to the workspace, and awaited his reply. He was right on target. Within a day I got a notice that he had posted the the completed work and awaited my review. It was golden. Not only did he clean up any issues of structure, he had reformatted my graphs and charts, had made recommendations for changes, and suggested some images to add. I quickly released the funds in escrow, and provided a very positive response.

Personal

I needed someone to help me organize my bills and accounts. While I can easily recommend how someone should organize themselves, I can sometimes be slack at doing it myself. So I posted the job on Elance (again, no upgraded listing), hammered out the specifics, and we were off. Within a day, I had a cadre of people offering to help. In this situation, I found someone in the US, that met the criteria I was looking for. In addition, they would set up everything and take care of my taxes at the end of the year as part of it. I requested further information as it dealt with my personal finances, and within a day they provided everything I needed. As this project is still ongoing, I can't provide you a happy ending, but I can tell you it is going great.

Value Your Time

A great way to begin using Elance is to look at your task list. Consider what you have for your hourly rate of time with others. For example, let's say you value your time at $30.00/hour. One of the tasks on your list easily requires three hours to do it. At $30.00/hr, it would be $90.00 for you to do the task. Say someone bids on the project to it for you at $50.00 for the entire task (you can specify whether you want to be billed at an hourly rate or flat rate… I usually go with flat rate.) Simple math tells you it would be better to bid this project out. As you go down your task list, you begin to see where you can outsource and what you need to do yourself. Some tasks you may find require you to personally do it. Others may be easily outsourced. Doing this, at regular intervals, will help you streamline your time and take you off of tasks that eat away at your day.

I would suggest start simple. Try one project and see how it goes. You will find things you will need to improve on and ways you can get better bidders. Build out from there and expand your project listings. As I said earlier, I have been using Elance for years, and it has taken a load of work off of me. So what are you waiting for?.

I thought it'd be helpful to compile a list of resources— consisting of books, tools, blogs, links, and guides which have helped me learn to brand myself, build an extensive network, travel around the globe, and design a business that I can run from anywhere in the world.

Enjoy!

Required Reading

· *Four Hour Work Week by Timothy Ferris*. Excellent book for streamlining your work and time. Definitely a must read.

• *How to Find a Job Teaching Online by Patricia Tobin, PhD*. This is a great book that walks you step by step on how to start teaching online. It offers a variety of resources as well.

• *Make Money Teaching Online: How to Land Your First Academic Job, Build Credibility, and Earn a Six-Figure Salary by Danielle Babb*. The title sounds a bit cheesy, but an excellent book.

• *Teaching Online: A Practical Guide by Susan Ko.* Excellent resource to have on your shelf.

• *Location180.com.* Sean Ogle really has nailed down living the remote lifestyle. I highly recommend following his blog and bookmarking it.

• *JimKukral.com.* Jim is an incredible resource for marketing and building an online presence. He offers a number of resources as well to get you started.

• *ThrillingHeroics.com.* Cody McKibben has an amazing blog on lifestyle entrepreneurship. Definitely bookmark this, as he provides a number of resources to help.

• *MindtheBeginner.com.* Looking for ways to minimize or streamline your life. This blog is for you.

Build Your Business and Online Presence

• *Bluehost.* Excellent hosting service. A bit pricey (about $100.00/yr.) but solid service, very little downtime, and great customer service and tech support.

• *Elance.* I would highly recommend getting an account here. Set up an account and post one job to get used to it. Even if you cancel it before it closes, you should at least try it. A must have website for building your staff. It is free.

• *GoDaddy.* Great hosting and customer service. Make sure you google "Godaddy coupons" before paying. You will get substantial discounts.

• *WordPress.* This is a very easy and versatile system to work with. Has so many uses for a web presence. Already comes pre-installed on many of the hosting companies I recommend.

Gadgets and Gear for Academic Free Agents

• *Aspire One.* Very cost-effective netbook and extremely light for traveling. • *Eddie Bauer Adventurer Pack.* I have been using this pack for years. Great for storing

your laptop and takes a beating. Also, comes with a lifetime guarantee. I've used it and they will replace it.

- *Motorola Droid 2*. This is the phone I use. Excellent for sturdiness, has both onscreen and pull out keyboard. Can't kill it. Believe me... I've tried.

International Communications and Scheduling

- *Awayfind*. Excellent tool for email when you are away from your computer. Only sends important emails to your phone text message.
- *Gmail*. Seriously? Are you still using Outlook?
- *Google Voice*. Great free alternative to regular phone. Keep in mind, it will not work with many of the free conference calling systems.
- *Ringcentral*. Excellent source for putting your phone, fax, and conference calls in one place and on the web. A number of resources are available in one package. Give the trial a try.
- *Skype*. This is widely accepted as an international means of communications.
- *TimeDriver*. Unless you want a lot of phone calls at all hours of the day or night, put this to use. You will be glad you did.

Invoicing, Distribution, and Shopping Carts

- *Paypal*. Very easy to set up an account and works great for invoicing, charging, and securely maintaining your online transactions.

Online Marketing and Promotion

- *Aweber*. Great for building distribution lists and email lists. Very easy to get up and running. Try the free version for 30 days, then upgrade.
- *Cafepress*. This is a great way (and easy way) to build your market following or to reward students.

Money and Personal Finance

- *Mint*. Consolidate your finances all in one place. This also has a nice phone app to help manage things while mobile.

Travel and Lifestyle

- *Dreamline Worksheet*. Excellent for framing out what you want to do with your free time.
- *Freecycle*. This is a great group to help you with cleaning out. Must sign up by county.
- *Ideal Lifestyle Costing by Tim Ferriss*. This is a great starting point for launching your new lifestyle.

Tools for the Academic Free Agent

- *Goldmail*. Very easy system to set up YouTube type presentations for your classes. Upload PowerPoint or create them natively. You can then add voice over.